THIS BOOK HAS BEEN COLORED IN BY

....

April 15 1966
Great young internationals. New plastic territory. From New York: sharp white fluorescent jacket, high yoke, low belt, silver buttons all the way. By Betsey Johnson, at Paraphernalia. Her clothes will be at branches of Bazaar from the end of April. Glasses, Oliver Goldsmith.

VOGUE

GOES
POP

COLORING
BOOK

IAIN R. WEBB

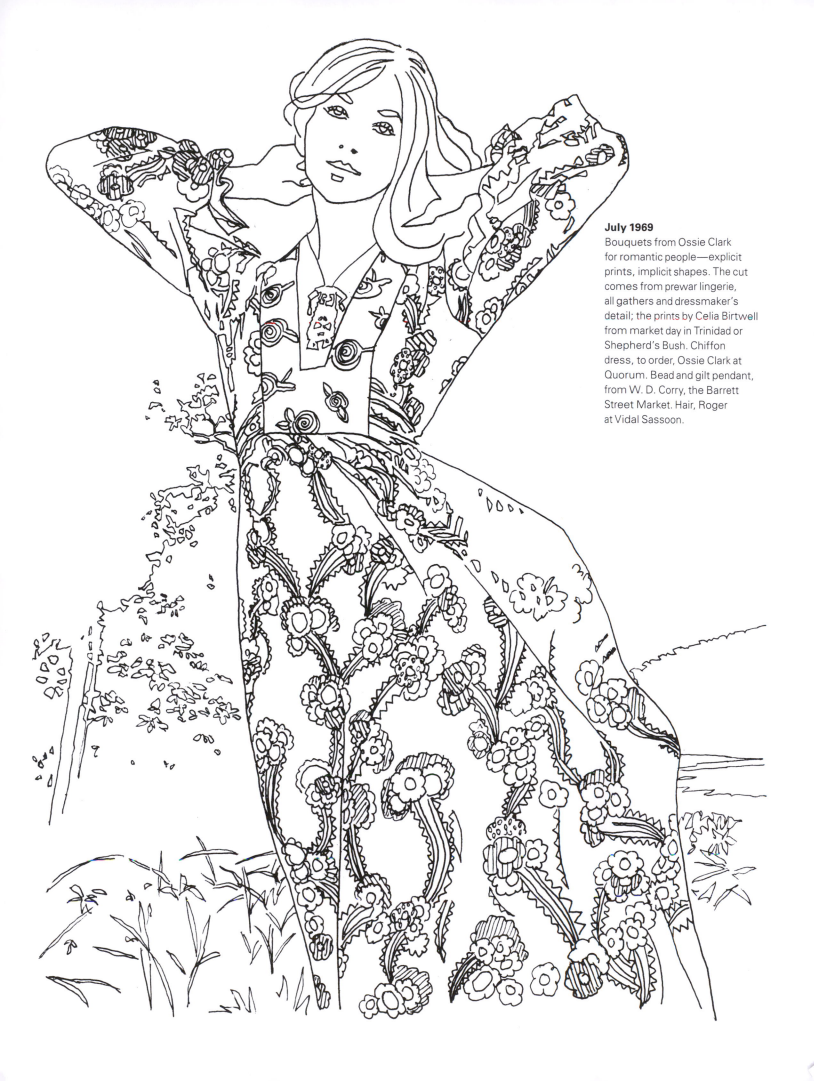

July 1969
Bouquets from Ossie Clark
for romantic people—explicit
prints, implicit shapes. The cut
comes from prewar lingerie,
all gathers and dressmaker's
detail; the prints by Celia Birtwell
from market day in Trinidad or
Shepherd's Bush. Chiffon
dress, to order, Ossie Clark at
Quorum. Bead and gilt pendant,
from W. D. Corry, the Barrett
Street Market. Hair, Roger
at Vidal Sassoon.

I am thrilled to, once again, have the opportunity to collaborate with British *Vogue* magazine. For *Vogue Goes Pop* I have focused on the 1960s, a decade I experienced through my sister, Mary's wardrobe. Throughout the decade she moved from beatnik black mohair and white lipstick to swirling rainbow-colored Op Art prints stitched into shockingly short shift dresses that she made herself. She was my original fashion icon.

The 1960s was the era when everything collided—youth, music, art, celebrity, politics, and, of course, fashion. It was a time of seismic change. Teenage girls grew up into independent young women who no longer wanted to dress like their mothers, so a fresh crop of young female designers dreamt up new dresses (and more) for them to wear. These designers included Kiki Byrne, Mary Quant, Marion Foale, Sally Tuffin, Barbara Hulanicki, Gina Fratini, Janice Wainwright, and Jean Muir in London, Betsey Johnson in New York, and Emmanuelle Khanh in Paris,

While the Beatles went from the nursery rhyme simplicity of "Love Me Do" to the complex, experimental anthem "Lucy In The Sky With Diamonds", fashion transformed from simple, bold silhouettes in bright colors, stripes, spots, and graphic florals to wildly bohemian get-ups cut from Paisley patterns and psychedelic prints inspired by trips to far flung destinations.

There were also the fantasy fashion heroines plucked from romantic yesteryear storybooks who wore a mad mix of rich Victorian velvets and lace, sumptuous oriental silks, and Indian brocade. *Vogue* called them the Ornamentalists and photographed them in front of a sunset in Sardinia or against temples in Sri Lanka. "A present-day Scheherazade", declared one *Vogue* editorial featuring Liberty textiles designed by Bernard Nevill, inspired by Turkish tiles and Persian carpets.

At the other extreme, shiny new stars needed shiny new clothes formed from PVC and metallic plastics, part inspired by the ongoing Space Race between the Russians and Americans that spanned the decade—Russia put the first man in space in 1961, the Americans landed on the moon in 1969.

These new fashions were modelled in *Vogue* by Twiggy, Jean Shrimpton, and Grace Coddington (who later joined the *Vogue* team as a fashion editor), while pop stars and actresses such as Julie Driscoll and Daliah Lavi were featured in the magazine and lauded for their original style.

As a teenager I painted pictures of Twiggy, so it felt only right that she appear on the cover of this book. Twiggy, who was declared "The Face of 1966", was an avid fashion fan. "Clothes were my passion", she recalls in her autobiography. "We would club together at school to buy *Vogue*".

So, enjoy revisiting the decade that gave fashion the mini-skirt, the discotheque dress, kinky boots, and the craziest of color combinations. "Once it was unacceptable to dress loudly", said *Vogue* in 1964. "Today's fashion ingredients have changed all that." I hope that you will find the far-out designs featured in *Vogue Goes Pop* a recipe for some fab coloring fun.

— *Iain R. Webb*

September 1 1967
GRAPHIC EFFECTS. Graphic new cape shape, by Cardin. Sharp like a cut out. Precision striped brown, white, and brilliant blue. With an asymmetrical collar, zip one side. Thigh-high boots, brown center-striped with black. Brown felt helmet with clear vinyl mask. Wool by Natier. Lipstick, Cardin's no 15.

→ **March 15 1965**
LE STYLE ANGLAIS '65. Head start to the new London Collections—dashing silk twill turban by Graham Smith for Michael. Stunning white, sizzling big black spots, a big beautiful butterfly bow. Make up by Cyclax: Amber Velvet GlamOtint foundation; Golden Haze powder. Lipstick, the new, sunny Honey Kiss by Cyclax.

7.

October 15 1965
WET LOOKS. Shining bright white with special bits and pieces, thunderbolt proof. Lightening flash of vinyl. Shiny stride of white, zipped up to a high collar. Coat by Mary Quant for Alligator, Harrods. Unsquare black handbag, vinyl and perspex, by Sally Jess, Top Gear. White lacy stockings, Women's Home Industries. Boots, Giusti. Black kid gloves by Kir, John Lewis.

→ **June 1963**
The beauties in BATH. Beautiful proof that Bath is the best-planned English city: the noble Crescent where façade matches façade but inside, each house is planned differently. *Left*: a simple silk shift in red with black dots. *Right*: Pale gray wool gently flared, with black and white silk cuffs and collar. Both at Deliss. Sunglasses, Oliver Goldsmith.

April 15 1965

Sun speed: everything gives. Stripes, checks, stretch, for this summer's beach life. *Left*: white stretch cotton and Helenca striped in black, Bib front, bare back, tie straps. *Right*: Stretch cotton and Helenca again, navy checked with red. Skirt slightly flared, top bare at the sides. Both by Sportsplage, at Biji Boutique. Cotton sun hats at Herbert Johnson.

→ **October 1 1967**

A slip of white jersey, with long fringed sleeves, fringe across the shoulders too. Foale & Tuffin; Harvey Nichols. Pendant and bracelet, John Jesse, Kensington Church Street. Tights, Sunarama, Fifth Avenue.

← June 1964

Cuff-frilled shift of pale blue voile lined with blue silk: flowers and fruit in tan and blue scattered all over. The rouleau band round the neck and sleeves, sharp dark brown. The scarf, all part of the bargain. By Hilary Huckstepp for Liberty. Location: the well-known Grenadier at Knightsbridge.

March 15 1967

BEARDSLEY AFTER A FASHION. Dramatic silk shift. Deep iris-blue on white with flowers whirling straight from Tannhauser. Mimi di N's earrings, to order Dickins & Jones. Adrien Mann's rings, Army & Navy Stores. Dress by Chloé, at Fortnum & Mason. Hair by Michael, make up by Gordon, at Leonard.

February 1967
All separate shape for a dress
with navy, short sweater top,
bold and curving bands of
white, a slight shaped white
skirt. By Avagolf. Ken Lane's
red, blue, and green enamel
bracelets. Wolsey's stockings,
at Selfridges. Navy patent shoes
slung back to a clear perspex
heel, at Charles Jourdan.

→ **April 15 1967**
Dandy suit to be worn with
long legs, in a super cotton
seersucker. Bright black
scattered with innumerable
yellow-centered pink daisies,
ditto wooden buttons. Rakish
long jacket with slanting
pockets and a matching pocket
handkerchief. Short and
marvellous cuffed shorts, at
Marrian-McDonnell. Primrose
Cacharel shirt, at Maxine
Leighton. Pink tights by Mary
Quant, at Miss Selfridge.

← October 15 1967
Racy winter looks...nifty
navy blue velour cape,
seamed and circling well into
line over matching culottes,
at Wallis. Navy blue six-foot
muffler, felt hat, Herbert
Johnson; Quant's tights, Bazaar;
Dents gloves, at Way In. Black
boots, at Ravel. And Austin
de luxe Mini, with optional
extras, at the Kenning Car Mart,
Hampstead Road, N.W.1.

October 1 1964
Spinning in now—the
discotheque dress, short,
sharp, and sparkling—gleam
and glitter yoked dress in wool
sparked all over with silver Lurex.
By Foale & Tuffin, at Woollands.
Crepe sling-back shoes, at
Russell & Bromley. Christian
Dior stockings without seams
on the heels. Hair, Gerard
Austen of Carita. Lipstick,
Coty's French Spice,

October 1 1969
Bronze leaf frock coat, a fabulous
sweep of curtain brocade with
black toggles, wide lapels under
a fringed woollen Russian
shawl printed. Coat, from Biba.
Shawl, from The Russian Shop.
Great chocolate velvet hat,
Christian Dior Chapeaux. Pale
gold crushed velvet pants, at
Emmerton Lambert, Chelsea
Antique Market. Scroll-worked
boots, to order, the Chelsea
Cobbler.

March 1 1967

International Collections: Spain. This spring's new look of navy blue and white and the three-piece rethought—pinafore dressing by Pertegaz. Young, dashing, superbly tailored. Short and smooth pinafore skirt, pure and simple military coat, both navy blue wool. Cool white see-through blouse, fishnet stockings, and straw cap. All hair by Duran of Carita, Madrid.

19

← **October 1 1963**

First of the watertights: rustic red raincoat of shiny PVC, shaped like a shirt, stitched in black. Mary Quant, at Bazaar. Matching hat, stitched in black, by James Wedge. Rolex GMT-Master, Garrard. The natural complexion basically Sun Tonic, by itself, without powder, with Tan Tone lipstick and nail varnish. All by Helena Rubinstein.

February 1966

New shine to Irish entertaining. Young and feminine looks—long and light yellow dress with white top, raised waist, ankle length, checked skirt. Donald Davies, from Mary Davies, London. White shoes, with black geometrics from Charles Jourdan. Black and white earrings, by Adrien Mann, from Fenwick. Hair by Gillian of Andre Bernard.

May 1967
Billowing milkmaid dress,
fresh-as-a-daisy orange and
pink green-stemmed flowers
on ploughed-field brown
woven cotton. Delicious puffed
short sleeves, tiny straight
but not laced bodice, and then
voluminous gathers all the way
round. High vamped, curvy
heeled, flower-printed shoes
to match. Dress, shoes, at
Biba, Kensington Church
Street and Brighton.

→→ **June 1969**
NEW NIGHTDRESSING. LIGHT,
WHITE, AND LACY. Blossoming
cotton lace negligée, partially
covering slightly suspended
nightdress. Both with a scalloped
edge. By Sinclair, from Liberty.

June 1965
Navy blue and white have a new clarity this summer, cotton a new crispness. Powerhouse zig-zags, electric pattern on a beach playsuit made to dazzle, not shock. Shorts shaped with a long front zip, smashing hood, and long-cuffed sleeves. *Vogue* Patterns 6491. Super white superman glasses, Olivia Goldsmith, from Susan Handbags.

→ **March 15 1967**
Bright and pretty short tent dress. Softly shaped, softly gathered round the neckline and wrists. Emerald green dotted with pink. In cotton voile, by Shubette, at Miss Selfridge.

January 1965
Persian flower garden design dating from 14th century. Silk Jamaica shorts worn with a chiffon smock lined from the yoke; harem sleeves. By Jane & Jane. Hat, in same silk, by James Wedge to order. All at Liberty. The ties from the hat are plaited into the hair. Hoop earrings, at Paris House. Lipstick, Nearly Pink by Cutex.

→→ **January 1966**
Snowproof, windproof, and looking very Russian. In fact, clothes with the same mood as those Julie Christie and Rita Tushingham will be seen wearing in the film of *Dr Zhivago*...long overblouse, by David Bond for Outback. New longer skirt, at Tony Armstrong Boutique. Big fur helmet, at Herbert Johnson. Boots, at Deliss.

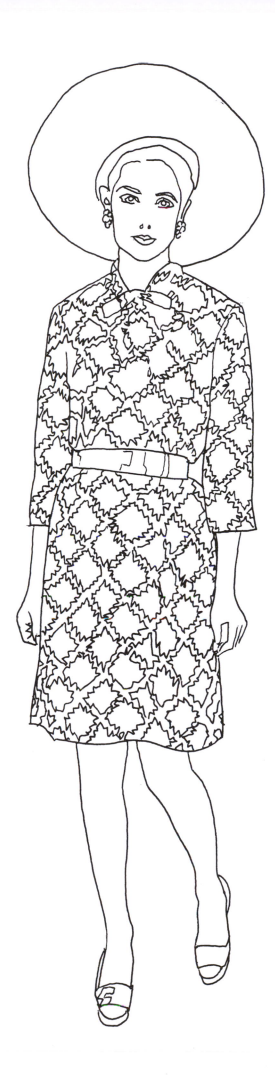

← October 15 1967
YOUNG IDEA'S GREEN BELT
GIRL. Capacious cape, circle of
pretty squares of bracken brown
and beige tweed, shaped into an
easy hood, double stitched, and
face framing. Look, no hands.
At Biba.

June 1967
SUBTLE SILKY DRESSES:
TWEED PRINTS. Lean black
silk dress, trellised with light
white ropes and tied with a pussy
bow. By Julian Rose, at Marshall
& Snelgrove. (We added the
black patent belt.) Black straw
hat, at Christian Dior London.
Kir's kid gloves. Vivier's black
patent platform sandals,
Rayne, Bond Street.

March 1 1966

YOUNG IDEA strides ahead. *This page*: Wasp stripe dress, thin black line; John Bates for Jean Varon, 17 Woodstock Street, London; Wallis, all branches. Shoes from Palisades. *Opposite*: Skinny coat-dress, stripy too; Veronica Marsh. 1 Palace Gate, London. Shoes by Luini, from Russell & Bromley.

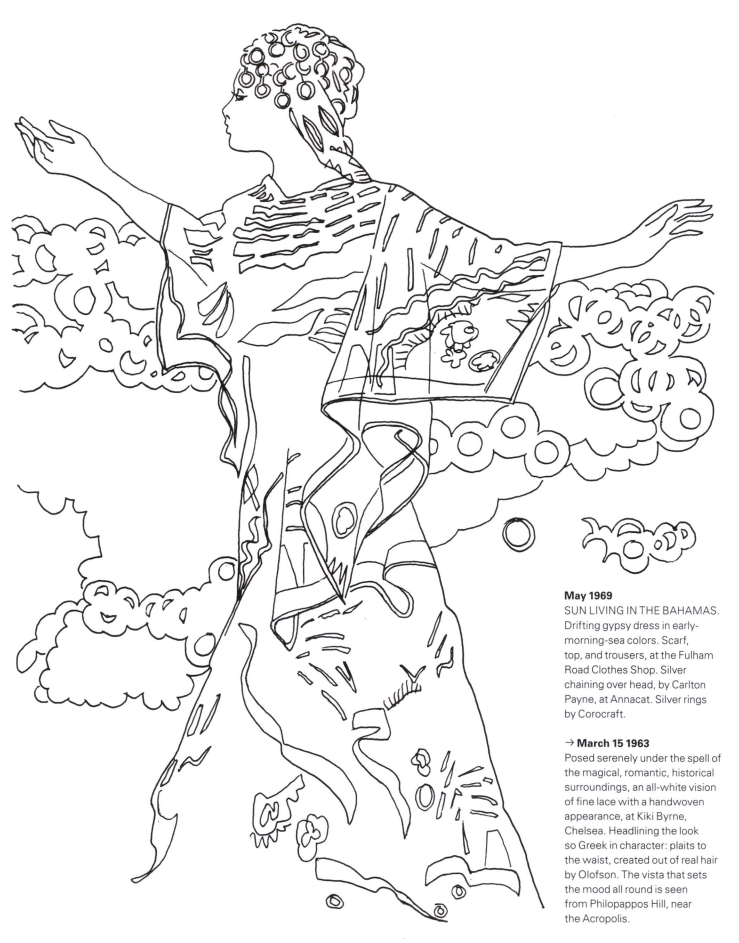

May 1969
SUN LIVING IN THE BAHAMAS.
Drifting gypsy dress in early-
morning-sea colors. Scarf,
top, and trousers, at the Fulham
Road Clothes Shop. Silver
chaining over head, by Carlton
Payne, at Annacat. Silver rings
by Corocraft.

→ March 15 1963
Posed serenely under the spell of
the magical, romantic, historical
surroundings, an all-white vision
of fine lace with a handwoven
appearance, at Kiki Byrne,
Chelsea. Headlining the look
so Greek in character: plaits to
the waist, created out of real hair
by Olofson. The vista that sets
the mood all round is seen
from Philopappos Hill, near
the Acropolis.

← October 15 1962

Velvet trim with white, tweed hat; black velvet suit scarfed and bound with grosgrain, worn with a man's tucked evening shirt. Suit by Marcus, at Dickins & Jones. Shirt, at Simpson. Checked hat, with a patent leather rose stuck through it, by Peter Shepherd, at Woollands. For theater, dinners: remove hat, button up the suit. The rosy lipstick, Tangee's Pink Mist.

March 15 1964

The rain it raineth every day. *Vogue* found the very best raincoats, the ones that look as though they're streaming before they even leave home. White raincoat fastened with gilt snaps, Weathergay, Harvey Nichols Little Shop. Aviator's cap, at the James Wedge Boutique, Vidal Sassoon. Boots, the Bally Boutique.

January 1968
Bare and beautiful, sun and moon dressing. Sunset views of Sardinia and sunset-and-after harem dress. Barest little top scooped low and lattice tied at the back, billowing trousers, in silk chiffon, to order from Savita. Hair by Alexandre. Lipstick, Estée Lauder's Agean Coral.

→ **December 1969**
A Christmas look to treasure by Pablo at Elizabeth Arden. The make up: Almost Beige Illusion foundation with Transparent Powder and Frosty Bronze Creme Blush. Gold-embroidered organza dress with matching trousers and veiling, to order from Belinda Bellville; framed with a gold, diamanté necklace, to order, from Ken Lane. Ring by Frances Beck & Ernest Blyth, at Garrard.

← **July 1966**
New cotton catch for beachcombers. Clear brilliant prints from the Pacific, bare, simple desert island dressing. Vivid Batik cotton sarong from Java. Wrapped round and round, in coconut brown and sand white, at Liberty's Oriental Shop. Castaway hair, blonde Dynel entwined with flowers, by Leonard.

March 1 1967
Checked to match. Sleeveless dress and straightforward jacket in smooth checked tweed, all pale pink, palest stone on clear blue horizon. By Dorville, at Liberty. Stone blonde straw panama, by Vendôme, at Fenwick. Bonnie Doon's stretching crepe stockings, at Bazaar. Kir's suede gloves, at Dickins & Jones.

April 15 1966
EYE VIEW of this summer's
looks. On a clear day you can
play forever...sailor's suit with
clear stripes of vinyl and plastic.
By Victoire for Hauser Sport.
93—97 Regent Street, W.1.
Glasses from Meyrowitz, Old
Bond Street, London, W.1.

September 15 1962

Les SNOBS! They choose their clothes with a wisdom beyond their years: good, well-made clothes that frilly blouses have been bypassed to buy! The black suede trench coat, double-breasted. The V-neck black leather coat, both by the Howard Manufacturing Co. The sweater, by John Laing. All clothes from 21 Shop, Woollands.

February 1963
HOW TO STRETCH THE
FASHION POUND. It's done—
like all conjuring tricks—by
creating an illusion; the illusion
being knits that look like a million
dollars. In fact the prices...
wouldn't entirely wreck the
shakiest bank account. Camel-
colored sweater-dress and
cardigan with gilt buttons.
Hogg of Howick, at Liberty.

→ **March 15 1965**
ADD CLOTHES AND STIR.
Strappy sandals, spiced with
stones: light and airy new shapes
right in step with the pale and
pretty new way of dressing.
Both sandals, Russell & Bromley.
Printed cotton voile jumpsuit;
floating and fragile, very, very
feminine. The print blurred,
tawny and beautiful, spiced
with blue and green. By
Frank Usher, Woollands.

← **January 1968**
YOUNG IDEAS LOOK AHEAD. The Fool are four: Josje, Marijke, Simon, and Barry, and the designs they make fantastic...a magician's impression of texture and color. *Left*: Sun velvet coat. *Center*: long dress with a waistcoat of brocade. *Right*: Sunset red velvet coat, with a cape. All by The Fool at Apple. Blue shoes, at Elliotts.

February 1967
PLAYING THE BLUES... AND NIGHT. Dark crepe culotte dress with curving camisole top, deep U back, and brilliant rhinestone buckled belt. By Susan Small. J.W.Benson's sapphire and diamond bracelets. Silvery glittery mules, at Magli. Tovar Tresses' blue Dynel hair arranged by Harold Leighton.

← **October 15 1967**
Simple shepherd's smock, in bright old-fashioned marmalade Harris tweed, the collar faced with checks. Wear it as an extra short coat, or over checked trousers. By Gina Fratini. Smoky apricot Shetland sweater, from Scott Adie, and ribbed knee-socks, by Adler, over pale rust tights, by Pex, at John Lewis. Ginger laced shoes, at Ravel.

September 1 1965
NEW COVER STORY FROM ALL OVER. Great new cover-ups— wrapped poncho; tent coat, high new flare. Poncho panther coat by Barocco, wrapped over tweed. The total look: marvellously covered up with the tweed dress hooded, tight sleeved, and matched by the hat.

November 1964
Nowadays if you can't think of
a thing to say your clothes can
speak for you. ZING frillup
KONK Clop. Fifty decibels of
satin cork-screw curls zinging
through the air, and tiers of
satin-bordered chiffon frolicking
against each other. Both by
Nettie Vogues. Konking satin-
covered bracelet, Adrien Mann,
Fenwick. Clopping black crepe
sandals, Russell & Bromley.

→ **October 1 1965**
Pale new sparkle, simple shapes
very dressed up. *Left*: Gold
Lurex crepe dress. White tweed
cardigan with gold and diamond
buttons. All at John Cavanagh
Boutique. Lame mules by Taj,
Savita. *Right*: chiffon blouse,
tweed skirt, at Carole Austen, 44
Sloane Street. Golden necklaces;
embroidered velvet cap, all at
Savita. Gold paillette mules, by
Hetty Bradley. Lipstick for both,
Lancaster's Rose Jacinthe.

← February 1969

Falls of fringes, white shining jersey, showers from the tight bodice and sleeves, slippery Tricel jersey dress in one with trousers. By Janice Wainwright for Simon Massey, Dickins & Jones. Forever silk scarf with fringes, Fulham Road Clothes Shop.

October 15 1966

Action suit for the space-age girl breaking new ground without nostalgia (although, perhaps, early lady flyers would have liked a prototype). Silver lamé elasticated for a skinny jacket, slim trousers, and skull cap. Jacket and cap, trousers, at Jaeger, Regent Street. Silver kid knee boots, to order, at Anello & Davide. Shiny silver matching visor, by Oliver Goldsmith.

← February 1967

Sailor navy, with white too. Criss-crossing checks angled round the middle on a little wool suit. Plain color reversing on a flying tent coat. By Harry B. Popper, Harrods. Otto Lucas white felt hat, at Fortnum & Mason. Wolsey's white fishnet stockings, at Selfridges. Flat bowed navy shoes, Miss Rayne, at Rayne, Old Bond Street.

February 1963

THE GREAT WHITE WAY. The something blue...is a pale blue sash: the something new is the dress itself—newer now in its power for flattery, newer in the simple way it takes the limelight. For a country or garden wedding, this broderie anglaise shirt-dress, and the fresh organdie headsquare, both by Muriel Martin, Liberty.

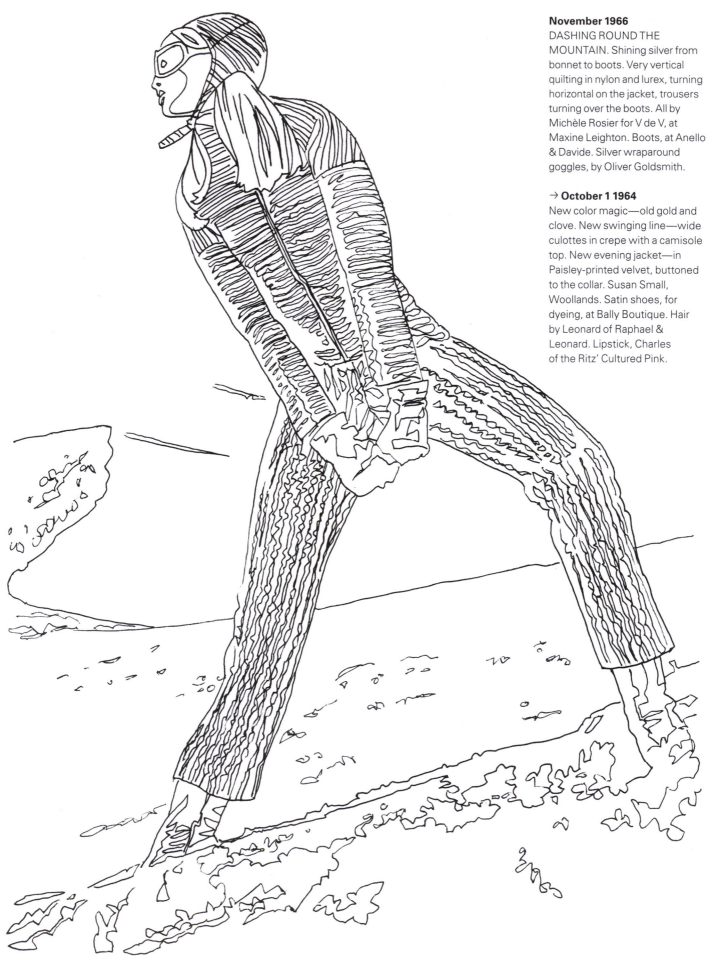

November 1966
DASHING ROUND THE
MOUNTAIN. Shining silver from
bonnet to boots. Very vertical
quilting in nylon and lurex, turning
horizontal on the jacket, trousers
turning over the boots. All by
Michèle Rosier for V de V, at
Maxine Leighton. Boots, at Anello
& Davide. Silver wraparound
goggles, by Oliver Goldsmith.

→ **October 1 1964**
New color magic—old gold and
clove. New swinging line—wide
culottes in crepe with a camisole
top. New evening jacket—in
Paisley-printed velvet, buttoned
to the collar. Susan Small,
Woollands. Satin shoes, for
dyeing, at Bally Boutique. Hair
by Leonard of Raphael &
Leonard. Lipstick, Charles
of the Ritz' Cultured Pink.

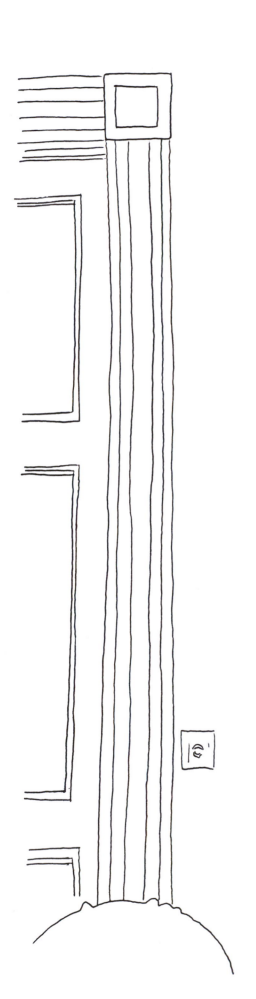

← ← **January 1967**
FASHION PURE AND SIMPLE.
Very simple country plot—
fashion naturals cut with ease
and dash, made in warm practical
fabrics, grass-root colors. Very
natural country cover story,
saffron-yellow hooded felt
coat bound with suede. Bonnie
Cashin, small, medium, large,
Liberty. Stockings, Adler.
Ghillies, Rayne, Old Bond Street.

October 1 1967
Tiny slip of yellow velvet, long,
full sleeves gathered at the cuffs.
By John Bates at Jean Varon,
Harvey Nichols. Finest spun gold
glitter stockings, by Mary Quant,
D.H.Evans. Yellow velvet shoes,
to order, at Anello & Davide. Gold
and pearl locket and rings, from a
selection at The Golden Past.

June 1964
BEATON: FACES FROM SHRIMPTON. Jean in Spanish mood; the dress that depicted this flavor for Cecil Beaton—black crepe, ankle long, ruffled down the edge, by Mary Quant, at Bazaar. Her hairstyle that fits this Spanish context was created by Alan at Vidal Sassoon.

→ April 1 1968
Sweet powdered-blue satin organza transformed into the prettiest shirtdress of spring. Wide and romantic garden party hat, all natural leghorn straw tied up demurely with blue velvet ribbons and flowering with forget-me-nots, too. By David Sassoon for Belinda Bellville. Glowing Sun Beige make up by Elizabeth Arden. And hair in beautiful ringlets, Michael at Michaeljohn.

June 1965
COTTON LANDSCAPE: NAVY
BLUE AND WHITE PATTERNS.
Clear-cut dress, precision bound,
navy blue on white. *Vogue*
Pattern 6505. White slubbed
rayon, Marshall Fabrics, Bourne
& Hollingsworth. All enamel
flower jewellery, by Corocraft,
at Dickins & Jones. Hair by
Leslie at Raphael & Leonard.

→ **Sept 1 1969**
The coat reaches absolutely
opposite conclusions. Carosa's
conclusion, an absolutely brilliant
joke and the ultimate use for
knitting wools. Two coats dyed in
the color of every Mexican fiesta
that ever was and built from
throat to ankle by rib, by pearl, by
plain, by skein, and fringe. Wools
by Di Crosa. Suede boots by
Barilla. Hair by Alba & Francesca.

June 1964

There's a whole new range of hats that strike a whole new rapport with the clothes they head—they don't just quietly fill in a gap, they boost and enhance the complete picture of charm and dash. The close shape, the turban. In pink organza, Otto Lucas, at Fortnum & Mason. Bloused dress and jacket in silk shaded red, orange, and pink, at John Cavanagh Boutique.

→→ **May 1966**

Flying Pucci print; silk beach cover up, cut like a dhoti and slit to the waist. Matching thonged sandals and elasticated bikini, at Fortnum & Mason. Hairpiece, Gerard Austen. Setting: the ruined city of Polonnaruwa.

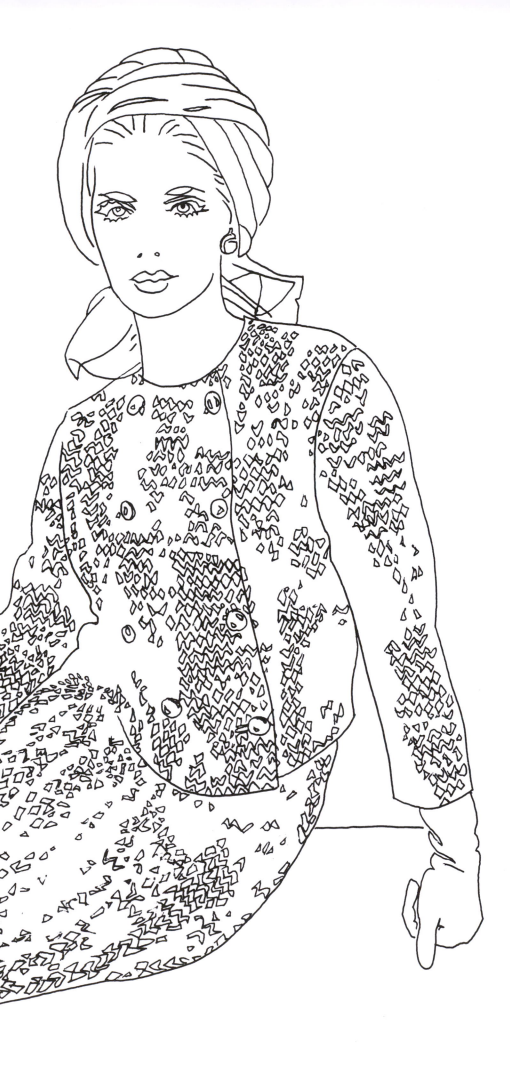

May 1967
Beautiful Ban-Lon seraglio separates, fine striped and plain. Long, lean, peppermint, pink, and lemon coat, brightly bordered with sequinned flowers, vents slashed high at the sides. Skinny striped vest top. And pretty plain lemon pajama trousers. By Ken Scott, at Fortnum & Mason. Giant earstuds, by Felicity Bosanquet for Adrien Mann. Hair by Ramon of Mark Ramon.

→ **October 1 1962**
White calf patterned with black giraffe spots for a sleeveless sweater. By Maggie Shepherd at Woollands. Center-parted shining hair by Raphael & Leonard. Translucent maquillage by Coty: Instant Beauty Satin Pearl. Rose Amaranth lipstick. Single-stone diamond rings, Jaeger-leCoultre watch, diamond necklace here worn as a bracelet, all by Kutchinsky. Jet ring at Paris House.

← April 1 1968

WAVES OF COLOR. Drop paint onto water, stir with a spoon and arrive at the random swirls and splashes of the new fabrics. Buy these stormy waves...and whip them into *Vogue* Patterns shirty shapes. In Liberty silk gauze. Shiny red Corfam belt, Paris House. Swirls of hair by Paul at Harold Leighton of Dorothy Gray. Lipstick, Coty's Rose Matazz.

March 1 1965

Knitwear international. Instant couture—jersey by Givenchy. Great name, great style, great debut...Givenchy jersey originals reproduced stitch for stitch for the first time in this country. Porcelain-blue dress, soft and fair, honeycomb textured. Turtle neckline wide in front, narrower at the back, by Givenchy. Jersey by Kilkenny, available at Harrods. Shoes, blonde leather cutouts, Charles Jourdan.

← April 15 1964

TOP PEOPLE. James Wedge has done more than almost anyone to bring hats into a young woman's life. He and Vidal Sassoon collaborate over a hat in the salon: you buy a hat, and the salon will do your hair to go with it. The latest extravaganza, a ravishingly pretty pink satin waterlily trailing satin petals like a waterfall, from the James Wedge Boutique at Vidal Sassoon, Bond Street. Lipstick, Orlane's Pétale.

November 1966

FAR AND AWAY THE BEST BUYS. Seafaring looks in new color currents, new print waves. Billowing harem pajamas with a neat polo-necked top. Covered all over with intricate twirls of pink, cream, and primrose. By Graham Price, at Miss Selfridge. Yellow earrings, by Rebe, to order at Maxine Leighton. Shoes by Taj, Rayne, Old Bond Street.

← **October 15 1968**
A tremendous investment, caught in white brocade, with vastly gathered sleeves, tall cuffs buttoned-up four times, a strict Mao collar, and detachable sash to tie in a butterfly bow, from Turnbull & Asser. Belt from Deliss. Gold cross and chain, from The Purple Shop, Chelsea Antique Market. White crepe trousers, by Ossie Clark, from Quorum. Hair by Michael at Michaeljohn.

September 1 1968
VALENTINO'S CHINA FIGURES. Photographed in Signora Agnese Bruguier's Palazzo Borghese apartment. Stately evening dress, Delft flowers and foliage, birds and butterflies, translated into heavy silk by Taroni. Porcelain make up by Gil of Max Factor. Hair by Alba & Francesca. Jewellery by Giovanna de Drago, among the wide selection at Debenham & Freebody.

← October 1 1965

Watch: supple metallic fabrics, new supple cloqués, gloves again. Lightening new gold and silver iced with white. Long evening coat of gold and silver lurex cloqué, collar and cuffs white fur. Smooth dress in cream corded silk. By John Bates at Jean Varon; coat, dress, Woollands; Darlings of Edinburgh. Diamante earrings by Christian Dior.

February 1969

Crisp new coat with the softest pattern—a big, blurry, beautiful watercolor plaid, sea-blue, chrome yellow on pure cream wool. By Mansfield, at Harrods. Creamy velvet hat, from Malyard. Sweater, by Munrospun, Town & Country Clothes. Cream leather gauntlets, by Kir. Cream mossy crepe tights, by Mary Quant. Little white shiny Living Skin boots, from Elliotts.

← **January 1968**
SUCCESS ISLAND SARDINIA.
Sun fashion success in Costa
Esmeraldan setting: Marisa
Berenson in Ken Scott's gypsy
dress of yellow poppies on
flame red. Ban-Lon jersey. Full
and springing from a narrow
waistband, long at the back,
shorter in front, from Fortnum
& Mason. Gold bracelets from
Fior. Hair by Alexandre. Lipstick,
Payot's Rosiris.

July 1968
She spells magic with the way
she sounds. She spells magic
with the way she looks—like a
melting statue...Julie Driscoll is
a London girl, oh yes...usually
wears old clothes, satin, velvet,
and lace. Here she wears satin
designed by Ossie Clark, and
printed in brown by Celia Birtwell
for Quorum. White slingback
shoes, at Ravel.

October 15 1966
EVENING DRESSING: A MATTER OF CHOICE. Variations on the silver theme. The long, silver, and white, ballooning and brocaded pajama dress. At Christian Dior. Earrings by Ken Lane. All hair by Michael at Leonard.

→→ **September 15 1964**
British achievements, 1964, start with a leading British export—Jean Shrimpton in scarf top and above ankle matching skirt in pure wool Liberty print. By Thocolette, Liberty. Earrings, K.J.L., John Cavanagh Boutique. Lipstick, Cutex' Nearly Pink. Hair by Leonard at Raphael & Leonard.

January 1967
THE GREAT FLOWER PLOT.
Bright blues and scarlet,
sunflower yellow and orange,
rich leafy green, all defined in
black, on an empire evening
dress. By Colin Glascoe. Adrien
Mann's blue ring, at Dickins &
Jones. Felicity Bosanquet's
larkspur flowered earrings, at
Marrian McDonnell. Hair by
Susan at André Bernard.

→→ May 1969
FRESH WOODS AND
PASTURES NEW. The first
landscape to wear, designed by
Bernard Nevill, worn by Twiggy...
over the hills and far away...
Bernard Nevill country, printed
on silks for Liberty. Culotte dress
with sash, trimmed in ric-rac
and white fringe, long scarf.
John Bates at Jean Varon,
Chanelle, Knightsbridge. Hair
by Leonard. Lipstick, Yardley's
Suki Pearl Red.

April 15 1966
Gunmetal gray on target. Lethal vinyl trouser suit for a fast life. V. de V. Rue Drouot, Paris. Violent violet angora shirt. Maxine Leighton, Conduit Street, W.1. Wellington boots, all branches Russell & Bromley.

March 15 1967
BEST BUYS GET THE FLOATING
VOTE. With free and easy
tent dresses in fine cotton and
light chiffons, made for now
and all summer through. Light
and brilliant cotton voile float.
Japanese pink, turquoise, and
orange. With winged sleeves cut
on the cross and floating free. By
Group 30, at Galeries Lafayette.
Turquoise suede shoes, from
Kurt Geiger.

October 1 1966
SOFT SPARKLE AND...
SCULPTURED GLITTER. Adding
new scope to evenings this
winter's two-texture story—
sculptured and geometric
satins and brocades, soft
and pliant silks and chiffons.
Gentlest trapeze shaping, long
gathered sleeves, silk organza
embroidered with daisies. Dress,
Vogue Patterns 6950. Organza
by Reichenbach, at Allans
of Duke Street. Suede mules
by Magli.

→ **June 1964**
The snap and ripple of white
piqué for a jacket with wide
curve of shoulder and billowing
back, a dress with cap sleeves
and gently tailored torso. Fabiani
Ready-to-Wear at Margray, from
Lucia, Berkeley Street. White
straw hat, Simone Mirman.
Kid gloves, Miloré.

October 1 1965
Dazzling new printing: golden blonde satin charmeuse lit with lacquer red velvet flowers. Long Eastern overblouse and trousers, at Christian Dior Boutique. Red enamel brooch, red mules with gilt heels, by Taj, at Savita. Lipstick, Dior no. 43.

→ **December 1968**
In Felix Harbord's golden drawing-room, rich in pillars, parrots, plush, and plinths, the most decorative features are the girl in the marigold crepe, by Dynasty, at Harrods, and Gervase, the pop singer, in his carpet-patterned dressing gown, from Mr Fish. Earrings, Ken Lane. Pale gold shoes with Maltese cross encrusted on buckles, Kurt Geiger. Rings from a selection at Hooper Bolton.

← **September 1 1965**
ITALY. Italian designers all
flocked to feathery looks for
great evenings. In full flight here,
a coat of coq feathers by Forquet.

May 1966
Savage beauty, Daliah Lavi,
Israeli actress...soon to make
The Spy with the Cold Nose.
Flaring chiffon robe, slit at the
back; golden Paisley patterning
on midnight blue; pale yellow
silk hipster trousers and bra
top, to order at Carole Austen.
Earrings, sandals of yellow and
orange glass beads, by Coppola
& Toppa, to order at Maxine
Leighton. Hair by Gerard Austen.

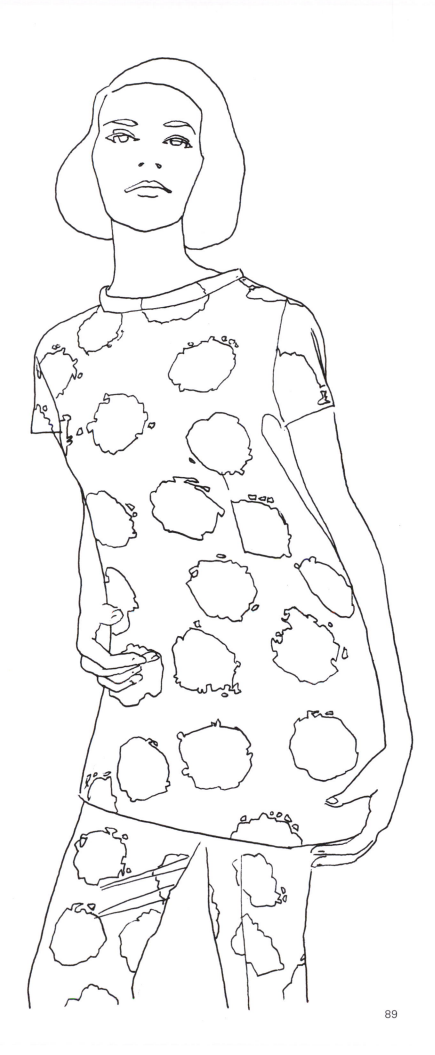

← **August 1969**
ART DECO'S SECOND
FLOWERING. Ice-cream flapper
dress in Neapolitan colors on
silk. By Leslie Poole. Pink silk
tights, by Twiggy Tights. Pink
satin shoes, at Anello & Davide.
Tasselled scarf, at Mr Fish.
Lipstick, Gala's Plain Scarlet.
Fabric designs, all from Bernard
Nevill's Jazz Collection, and satin
cushions from Liberty. Art Deco
wall frame from façade of Ideal
Standard House.

March 15 1964
LONDON LOOKS. JOHN
CAVANAGH carries his Thirties
mood into evening: beaded
dresses with low-cut bloused
tops, fluid lines; ethereal organza
or lace dresses; shantung or
crepe pajamas and tunic, the
tunic often embroidered. Black
and white silk crepe trousers and
tunic. Crepe, Bianchini Férier.
Hair by Gerard Austen of Carita.

September 1 1965
ITALY. Positive new evening
looks, smooth or shining,
clearly black and white. Shining
white gabardine and glittering
black and white embroidery by
Barocco. Jewellery by Petochi.
Evening shoes by Silvia of
Fiorentina. Setting: Countess
Volpi de Misurata's palazzo
in Rome.

September 1 1963
THE PARIS CLIMATE. A double-take on CAPUCCI'S play on the sportif. *Left*: a swashbuckling scarlet and collarless coat; a cream shifty dress; cobra shirt that pairs off with the bowler hat. *Right*: a high, lean, three-quarter stretch of coat; a sleeveless dress of wool crepe. A cloche of black velours. Exit lines for both: football socks.

April 1 1969
THE FRUIT SHERBETS. New slices of color: apricots, iced raspberry, blackberry, and lime. Lime dress in light knife-creased pleats, lime hat, and soft blackberry jacket, all iced in raspberry. To order from Belinda Bellville. Enamelled rhinestone bracelets, from Ken Lane. Domed diamond and tourmaline ring, from Andrew Grima. Hair by Michael at Michaeljohn.

→ **March 1 1968**
Valentino's memorable pretty evenings—airy white separates. Most feminine white lace pullover over lightly pleated georgette skirt. Again, a polo collar, narrow pearl-buttoned cuffs, and appliquéd white lace and blonde stockings—certainly the prettiest seen so far. Moiré shoes, by Dal Cò for Valentino.

January 1965
Scheherazade '65. The
legendary new prints designed
by Bernard Nevill. Odalisque
trouser suit in butterfly colors
from a 15th-century Caucasian
carpet. Chiffon bandit scarf
in the same staccato print.
Cushions, to order from Liberty.
Peacock-green bobble earrings,
from Dickins & Jones. Bangles,
Savita. Lipstick, Rose Blanc by
Lancôme. Hair by Gerard Austen.

→ **April 15 1969**
The new Tuscan look by Pablo
of Elizabeth Arden. With Sun
Bisque illusion foundation,
Transparent powder, Frosticotta
Creme Blush, and Sheer Frost
highlights. With Extra Long
lashes, eyebrows brushed
upwards in fine feathered
strokes; Siena lipstick. The silk
is the Cornfields from Bernard
Nevill's dazzling new collection
of garden and landscape prints,
at Liberty, for scarf.